The Library of Explorers and Exploration

SIR WALTER RALEIGH

Explorer for the Court of Queen Elizabeth

Steven P. Olson

the rosen publishing group's
rosen central

To my mother, the educator, and my father, the sailor

Published in 2003 by The Rosen Publishing Group, Inc.
29 East 21st Street, New York, NY 10010

Copyright © 2003 by The Rosen Publishing Group, Inc.

First Edition 1821863

Library of Congress Cataloging-in-Publication Data

Olson, Steven P.
Sir Walter Raleigh: explorer for the court of Queen Elizabeth / by Steven P. Olson. — 1st ed.
    p. cm. — (The library of explorers and exploration)
Summary: A biography of Sir Walter Raleigh which examines his early life, his relationship with Queen Elizabeth, his desire to explore the New World, his defeat of the Spanish Armada, his quest for El Dorado, his life as a writer, and more.
Includes bibliographical references and index.
ISBN 0-8239-3631-7 (lib. binding)
1. Raleigh, Walter, Sir, 1552?–1618—Juvenile literature. 2. Great Britain—History—Elizabeth, 1558–1603—Biography—Juvenile literature. 3. Great Britain—Court and courtiers—History—16th century—Juvenile literature. 4. Explorers—Great Britain—Biography—Juvenile literature.
[1. Raleigh, Walter, Sir, 1552?–1618. 2. Explorers.]
I. Title. II. Series.
DA86.22.R2 O47 2003
942.05'5'092—dc21

                                                                    2001008534

Manufactured in the United States of America

CONTENTS

INTRODUCTION

A RENAISSANCE MAN

While serving in the war in Ireland in 1581, Sir Walter Raleigh received an order to capture Lord Roche, an Irishman whose loyalties to the English Crown had come under suspicion. Captain Raleigh was ordered to lead his band of ninety men to Roche's castle, battle his guards, capture Roche, and return him to the English for questioning. However, Irish intelligence got wind of the plan. Thirteen hundred Irish soldiers were positioned between Raleigh and Roche's castle in order to ambush Raleigh.

Faced with an enemy this strong, what would Captain Raleigh do? A smart captain might find a way to avoid the mission. A bold captain might gather more men and attack the enemy. Yet this smart and bold captain found a better plan. At the head of a band of ninety men, Raleigh

Sir Walter Raleigh was one of the great characters of the Elizabethan Age. He made a name for himself fighting the Irish and later became a favorite of Queen Elizabeth I. He also organized expeditions to the New World, battled the Spanish Armada, served in Parliament, and wrote fine poetry on the side.

departed at ten o'clock at night, marched all night around the ambush, arrived at Roche's fort in the morning, warded off the attack by Roche's men, and captured the lord at breakfast. The next night, he sneaked back with the lord, losing only one man in the masterful mission.

Great glory, however, was to elude Raleigh, as Lord Roche proved to be a loyal subject of the English Crown and had no useful information on the Irish. For all of the risks he took, Raleigh's mission amounted to a failure. This pattern of success followed by failure repeated itself throughout Raleigh's life.

Using his wits, charm, and daring, Raleigh achieved many great successes and suffered terrible failures on the battlefield and in other arenas. Over the course of his life, Raleigh raised himself from humble beginnings to become the favorite in the court of the queen of England. Like an actor in many different plays, he succeeded by learning how to play different roles. At various times, Raleigh found himself playing the role of soldier, explorer, writer, gentleman, politician, and, finally, prisoner. A brilliant and courageous man, Raleigh plunged into each role with complete belief in himself and his abilities. He mastered some roles. Some roles mastered him.

1
THE BIRTH
OF THE INDIVIDUAL

Hereat the hardest stones were seen to bleed
And groans of buried ghosts the heavens did pierce.
—Sir Walter Raleigh's
"A Vision Upon This Conceit of the Faerie Queen"

Walter Raleigh is believed to have been born around 1554, into a family that had been farming in the area surrounding Devon, England, for a very long time. His father, also named Walter, could trace the family roots in the area back to 1066, when William the Conqueror and his Norman soldiers invaded. The ground around Devon was stained with the blood of heroic defenders and invaders, and steeped in the fresh air that blew in off the Atlantic Ocean. It is into this tradition of glory on the sea that one of England's true Renaissance men was born.

Sir Francis Drake.

From an Original in the Sydenham Family.

*His Seal & Autograph from an original Letter
in the Possession of John Thane.*

Raleigh's early life was hardly promising. Although his family was well-known and respected in the area, it had fallen on hard times. Fortunes made by earlier generations had been wasted away, and the family no longer owned Hayes Barton, their simple, thatched-roof home.

By the time young Walter was born, there were many young voices in Hayes Barton. Both of Walter's parents had been married before. From an earlier marriage, Walter's father was connected to the Drakes, a local family. Walter's stepcousin, Francis Drake, would become one of England's finest explorers. Walter's mother had previously been married to Otho Gilbert and had three sons with him: John, Humphrey, and Adrian. Humphrey would play a significant role in Walter's later life.

The couple had already had one son together. According to the laws of inheritance, the eldest son received everything after his parents' deaths, and Walter's older brother, Carew, stood to inherit what little the family could offer. For Walter, his father could provide only introductions to important people in the area, who might help him build a successful future.

Sir Francis Drake, Walter Raleigh's stepcousin and contemporary, was a distinguished explorer and English admiral. Drake was born into a poor family and he went to sea at the age of thirteen. His outstanding skills soon won him fame and wealth, especially for his daring raids against Spanish colonies in the New World. He became a national hero and one of Queen Elizabeth's favorites for his role in the defeat of the Spanish Armada.

In this 1870 painting by John Everett Millais, a young Walter Raleigh is enchanted by a sailor's tale of adventure at sea. Raleigh had interests in many areas of both the arts and the sciences. He is thought to have inspired the phrase "Renaissance man," which refers to a person who has broad intellectual interests and is generally well-rounded.

History of Devon

The sandy soil of Devon's countryside allowed for cultivation of some crops, but it mostly served as a region for shepherding and warfare. During the Middle Ages, a period that stretched from AD 350 to AD 1450, the area around Devon was conquered and reconquered by a variety of groups from all over western Europe.

The narrow peninsula that holds Devon and Cornwall is isolated from the rest of England, yet it has been subjected to numerous invasions. When the Romans landed there, they chose not to cross the hills that protected the peninsula. Later, the Saxons did come and pushed all the way to Cornwall, settling among the local people. Then came the Danes and the great Norman conqueror, William, in 1066. Blood was spilled and mixed and, by 1350, most of the towns in Devon and Cornwall were settled by peoples who had crossed great distances and survived battles along the journey.

The tradition of valiant conquest continued to feed imaginations until the time of Raleigh's birth. In old Celtic songs grew the legend of a mighty king, Arthur, who was reportedly born in an abbey in Cornwall, near Devon. Attached to the legends of King Arthur were the values of honor, truth, and the beauty of heroic defeat. One can imagine how these old stories, the history of the area, and the lure of the sea fed the dreams of a young boy with an active imagination. One can see how such a child, who was not expected to amount to much, might look with longing westward to the sea and perhaps eastward to London, where the great changes of the Renaissance were happening.

The Renaissance and the Birth of the Individual

Out of the ashes of the warfare in the Middle Ages grew the Renaissance. Prior to the fourteenth century, much of Europe was organized into small states governed by tyrannical lords who held the land by intimidation and violence. The warlords fought for land and horses. It was a time of violence and destruction.

Over time, a few landlords were able to gain and hold much larger pieces of land, grow more crops, and trade the extra crops for spices, fabrics, and other materials. For them, life was no longer such a struggle. Goods and services could be purchased from other people for money, which was used to purchase goods and services again. Over a period of centuries, wealth trickled down from the landlords to a new group of merchants and craftsmen, the middle class. Landlords and merchants found that they had the luxury of time on their hands.

Sir Walter Raleigh

With free time, people began to dream about the arts and think about the sciences. This great flowering of arts, sciences, philosophy, and mathematics became a rebirth for Europeans. That rebirth is called the Renaissance. The Renaissance, which is French for "rebirth," is commonly believed to have started in Florence, Italy, in the fourteenth century, and then to have spread outward. All over Europe artists and inventors began making startling discoveries and works of art.

By the time of Walter Raleigh's birth, the Renaissance was in full bloom. Among the common-born people around him, he must have seen the possibilities of becoming an ambitious and daring individual. His older half brother, Humphrey Gilbert, had begun a career as a soldier and was having success in the wars in France. It was these wars between Protestants and Catholics that would draw Walter Raleigh from the shores of Devon into the larger world. As the Protestant movement grew in England, France, and the Netherlands, the struggle reshaped western Europe and the future that one bright-eyed boy saw for himself.

Sir Humphrey Gilbert, the founder of the first English colony in North America, was born about 1539 to Otho Gilbert, whose widow later married Walter Raleigh's father. In 1583, Gilbert invested his family's fortune into an attempt to found a colony in the northern part of North America. Gilbert landed at St. John's, Newfoundland, which he claimed for England, but farther south he met with repeated misfortunes. On the return voyage to England, he was lost at sea.

2

RELIGIOUS WARS IN FRANCE AND IRELAND

If in Ireland they think that I am not worth the respecting, they shall much deceive themselves. I am in place to be believed not inferior to any man, to pleasure or displeasure the greatest; and my opinion is so received and believed as I can anger the best of them.

—Sir Walter Raleigh

Before the reign of Henry VIII, England had been a Catholic country in good standing with the pope. However, for reasons having little to do with religious faith, King Henry broke with the Catholic Church to start a new one, the Church of England. This break started conflicts in Europe that lasted long after Henry's death. In one, the French Huguenot War, Walter Raleigh learned the rules of war and his role as a leader of Protestant soldiers.

King Henry VIII is most famous for his six marriages. In this painting, he is surrounded by his wives. Clockwise from the top, they are: Anne of Cleves (fourth), Katherine Howard (fifth), Anne Boleyn (second), Catherine of Aragon (first), Catherine Parr (sixth), and Jane Seymour (third). Henry had two of his wives, Anne Boleyn and Katherine Howard, executed on charges of adultery.

History of Protestantism in England

In 1509, at age eighteen, Henry became the king of England and married Catherine of Aragon. Despite Henry's desire to produce a male heir to the throne, his marriage to Catherine only produced a girl, Mary, in 1516. By 1532, Henry, then forty-one years old, found himself in a difficult situation.

He had fallen in love with another woman, Anne Boleyn. Perhaps she could produce his male heir, he thought. Yet he already had a family. The solution for Henry was to rid himself of his first wife. The archbishop of York attempted to secure an annulment of Henry's marriage to Catherine from Pope Clement VII. The pope happened to be under the influence of Emperor Charles V, who was the nephew of Henry's wife, Catherine. In the eyes of the Catholic Church, Henry and Catherine were married forever. To Henry, this was unacceptable.

Henry forced Parliament to write several laws that gave him complete control over religion in England. The pope saw Henry's actions as a threat to the Catholic Church. In 1533, to try to fix the problem, the pope agreed to Henry's choice for Archbishop of Canterbury, Thomas Cranmer who immediately declared that Henry and Catherine were divorced. Henry married Anne, who was quickly crowned queen of England. In response, the pope excommunicated Henry from the

Catholic Church. The battle lines between Henry and the Catholic Church were drawn.

In the same year, Anne gave birth to a child, Elizabeth, who would become the queen of England during most of Walter Raleigh's life. In the following year, the break from the Catholic Church was completed with the creation of the Church of England. King Henry, of course, was named its leader. As the leader of the Church of England, Henry continued to marry, divorce, and execute his wives. By the time Henry died in 1547, he had left a number of children, each with a claim to the throne, and a big mess for his country to solve.

Competition among the heirs was fierce: Edward VI ruled for six years and was succeeded by Mary, Henry's daughter by Catherine of Aragon. Mary imprisoned Elizabeth, her potential rival for the throne, in the Tower of London in 1554 after a revolt was launched against her.

Mary, a Roman Catholic like her mother, married King Philip II of Spain, who was also a devout Catholic. The Protestants in England rebelled against this marriage. A male offspring from this marriage would have further tied England to the Catholic Church, yet it was not to be. Mary died childless in 1558, and according to the laws of succession, Elizabeth, the legal heir to England's first Protestant king, became queen. Her coronation angered King Philip, who vowed for the remainder of his life to unseat her.

Within England, the presence of Elizabeth on the throne raised many questions. Who would she marry? According to royal law, her husband would become king of England and would rule the country. Her choice of husband was a very important decision for her, for her country, and for the religion into which she was born.

The Protestant Raleighs

King Henry and Queen Elizabeth used their political and economic power to build up the Protestant religion. In England, one's choice of religion was not a personal decision; it was a test of national loyalty and created much bitterness among Catholics. Acts of violence between Protestants and Catholics were common in the countryside. Titles and the rights to impose taxes were granted to individuals by royal decree, so people who wanted to gain advantages had to earn the favor of the Crown. One sure way to gain favor was to convert to Protestantism. Those who converted to Protestantism received generous benefits. Over time, Protestants took possession of most of the country's money, power, and land, while Catholics were largely left out.

In 1587, Queen Elizabeth executed her cousin Mary Stuart who had a claim to the throne of England. Urged by the pope, King Philip II of Spain *(pictured here)* vowed revenge for his fellow Catholic. Some believe he was also angered at Elizabeth's rejection of his marriage proposal. Between 1586 and 1588, he prepared a large fleet of 130 ships, known as the Spanish Armada, to invade England but was defeated by the English navy.

Born into the Protestant faith, Raleigh must have seen that the world around him was connected to his church. His father, a respected man in the community, was Protestant. Raleigh's large collection of cousins, who were gaining admission to college or military appointments, were Protestant. The greatest figure in the land, the queen, was Protestant.

Through family connections, Raleigh enrolled at Oxford University in 1569, but his stay there was short. In France, his relative, the Comte de Montgomerie, was leading the Protestant Huguenot rebellion against the Catholic Church. France was divided into regions controlled by one faction or the other. The nation was in turmoil, and there was no clear religious leader. The lure of fighting for his family, his religion, his country, and his queen must have been irresistible to Raleigh. When he was fifteen years old, he left school and entered the fray at the side of Montgomerie.

Raleigh in France

The fighting was brutal. In one of his first campaigns, Raleigh was at the battle at Montcontour in 1569, where 10,000 soldiers died. On Saint Bartholomew's Day in 1572, the Huguenots had come to Paris to celebrate a royal wedding, when the mother of King Charles IX ordered the assassination of Huguenot leaders, including Admiral Gaspard de Coligny and the

Protestantism Vs. Catholicism

During the sixteenth and seventeenth centuries, the wars between Protestants and Catholics spread across western Europe. In Raleigh's lifetime, the leaders of the various factions were as follows:

England
Protestant leader: Elizabeth I. Later, James I. Catholic leader: Mary Tudor until her death in 1558. Then, Mary Stuart of Scotland.

Spain
Protestant leader: none
Catholic leader: King Philip II

Netherlands
Protestant leader: Queen Elizabeth I of England
Catholic leader: King Philip II of Spain

France
Protestant leaders: Louis I de Bourbon, Admiral Gaspard de Coligny
Catholic leaders: Henri I de Lorraine, Catherine de' Medici, King Henry III

According to legend, Walter Raleigh charmed Queen Elizabeth by spreading his cloak across a puddle so she would not muddy her feet. While there is nothing to confirm this story, the fact that the cloak is included in Raleigh's coat of arms indicates that the incident may have actually occurred.

Comte de Montgomerie. The resulting violence left 3,000 Huguenots dead in Paris and another 10,000 dead in the surrounding country at the hands of Catholic mobs.

Raleigh kept fighting, and he was good at it. He had grown to over six feet tall and towered over most of his men. A natural leader, Raleigh was resourceful and sometimes brutal in battle. Raleigh and his troops trapped a group of Catholics in a cave and threw smoldering straw in to smoke them out. The men inside either died from smoke inhalation or ran out to die on the swords of Raleigh's men.

Although Raleigh valiantly led his men in France and enjoyed the thrill of battle, it did leave a painful impression on him. Years later, he reflected on the fighting in France in his *Historie of the World*, "The greatest and most grievous calamity that can come to any state is civil war." The conflict between what one must do and what one should do troubled him to his final day.

Raleigh in Ireland

By 1575, Raleigh was back in England and training for a new role as a lawyer. It was a profession he would never pursue. One day, according to legend, he encountered Queen Elizabeth, who had come to a puddle in her path. Quickly, Raleigh removed his elegant cloak and laid it down across the water so that the queen could cross without

For successfully suppressing Catholics who rebelled against Protestant rule, Queen Elizabeth I granted Raleigh 42,000 acres in Youghal, Ireland. He lived there in a stately house, Myrtle Grove *(above)*, built in the mid-sixteeth century. Although the house was later modified, it retains its original character and contains some interior features that probably date back to the 1580s. In 1585, Raleigh planted the first potatoes in Ireland in the gardens of Myrtle Grove, and historians believe that the house was the site of the first tobacco smoking in Europe.

getting her feet damp. Charmed, the queen took note of the dashing young soldier.

Born into a poor family lacking noble blood, Raleigh desired to rise in the eyes of his queen, and he needed a means to do so. England had conspired to regain control of Ireland since the fourteenth century. By driving Irish Catholics from their lands, the English could expand their Protestant empire and colonize Ireland with people who would raise crops in the name of the English Crown. Before England colonized the New World, Ireland was the land of opportunity, where an ambitious and resourceful man could silence the Irish Catholics and make a name for himself. Raleigh was such a man.

In the name of his Protestant queen, Raleigh campaigned against Irish Catholics with great success. As a soldier for his church, country, and queen, Raleigh fought with great daring against an opposition of far greater numbers. In the heat of the battle, he was often seen extremely calm, as if he did not fear death. Later, facing his own death, he retained that calmness and earned the respect of all who witnessed it.

Raleigh did become a successful captain in Ireland and led a number of victorious campaigns, including the daring capture of Lord Roche. With each success, Raleigh wrote to the queen's court of his conquests. While his letters were addressed to two of the queen's highest counselors, Lord Walsingham and the earl of Leicester, his real target was the queen and a role for himself in her court.

3

LIFE IN THE COURT
OF ELIZABETH I

He had in the outward man a good presence, in a handsome and well–compacted person; a strong natural wit and a better judgment, with a bold and plausible tongue, whereby he could set out his parts to the best advantage.
—Sir Robert Naughton, writing of Sir Walter Raleigh

When Walter Raleigh laid his cloak down for Queen Elizabeth, he began to play an exciting and dangerous game. Queen Elizabeth was the most powerful woman in Europe, and she was unmarried. Raleigh began to explore the very complicated game of love. In the Court of Queen Elizabeth, this game had special rules and hidden dangers. In it, Raleigh the gentleman emerged as a winner.

The Virgin Queen

When Raleigh met Queen Elizabeth, he was a dashing thirty-year-old man, and she was well past forty. Despite extensive negotiations, she had not found a man suitable to marry.

ELISABETHA
REG: ANGLIÆ.

Elizabeth I *(above)* ruled England from 1558 until her death on March 24, 1603. When Elizabeth was three, her father Henry VIII, had her mother, Anne Boleyn, beheaded for supposed adultery and treason. Despite her difficult childhood, Queen Elizabeth was renowned for her learning, regal majesty, and national pride. The latter half of the six-teenth century in England is called the Elizabethan Age because of Elizabeth's strong influence over society, culture, and conquest.

From the day she was born, her parents, King Henry VIII and Anne Boleyn, had looked for a suitable match. Over the course of many years, Elizabeth had met and been matched with a number of suitors who would have been acceptable heirs to the throne of England. Alas, all of them were rejected. Elizabeth never fell in love with any of the men who approached her, fearing they wanted the crown on her head rather than the love in her heart.

She longed for a stirring, romantic love. Over time, she found herself drawn to the soldiers and sailors who were part of the court around her. Her first real passion was directed at Robert Dudley, the earl of Leicester, whom she had known since she was eight years old. Elizabeth loved him for many years but never agreed to marry him. Finally, the earl turned his attention elsewhere and married another woman. Elizabeth repeated this pattern many times. She would pay attention to a young man and encourage his interest in her. When he insisted that they marry, she would reject him and begin again with another handsome, young man. Why did Elizabeth not want to marry any of her official suitors or the men whom she truly loved? There are a number of reasons.

When Elizabeth was three, her own mother was beheaded on the order of King Henry VIII, her father, supposedly for adultery. Five years later, her stepmother and Anne Boleyn's cousin, Katherine Howard, was also beheaded by King Henry. Clearly, these events would have made an impression on a young woman. According to law, Elizabeth's husband could become the king of England; if she married someone with his own claim to the throne, it would be possible for him to have her beheaded.

That man would rule England and the Church of England. To protect the nation that she dearly loved, Queen Elizabeth had to choose a king very carefully. Did her suitors want to take over England? Did they want to destroy Protestantism and the Church of England? Her suitors may have smiled, brought gifts, and enchanted her with loving words, but their real motives may not have been well-intentioned.

As Elizabeth grew older, she became very adept at evaluating her suitors. She had taken a torn country, unified it, and helped it to blossom among the growing empires of France and Spain. She was no fool, yet she also yearned for real love.

Raleigh and Elizabeth: The First Years

By the time he met Queen Elizabeth, Walter Raleigh's dark, chiseled face stood above the heads of others at court. Already, he had grown a deep brown beard that drew to a point below his chin, sharpening his hawkish features. To complement such a striking face, Raleigh wore elaborate jewelry and bright colors in bold costumes. Although he spoke with the strong accent of his native Devon, Raleigh's speech and manner suggested someone of great education and intellect.

This polished man had accomplished a great deal in the battlefields of France and Ireland. None of the other men at court could match Raleigh's intellectual ability. Witty and charming, Raleigh always managed to find the right thing to say at the right time. In addition to his unflinching courage and successes on the battlefield, Raleigh had an abiding interest in poetry, which Queen Elizabeth shared. As early as the age of twenty, Raleigh was writing and publishing well-regarded poems, for at the time soldiers who fought with passion were often the first tellers of the romantic tales of the battlefield. Raleigh had a natural ability to recall the facts of his explorations and to embellish them into grand stories.

Through his stories and poems and great personal charm, Raleigh impressed the queen. That he stood before his queen without fear or awe must have been very intriguing to her. Here, she must have thought, is an interesting man.

Raleigh and Elizabeth became very close. They shared favorite poems with each other. Raleigh began to write poems just for her. Eventually, Raleigh declared his love for her.

Even when he was a young man confined to a ship, Raleigh tried to look his best. Despite his low wages, Raleigh wore expensive clothes that made him appear to be a wealthy man. He wore the best gentlemen's styles of the time, giant lace collars, flowing capes, and jewel-encrusted jackets.

Raleigh was aware of the risks of this exploration of love. To be the queen's favorite was to acquire enemies who wanted to play the role of favorite, too. To be the queen's favorite and then to lose her friendship could cost him his life.

One night, he used a diamond to scratch a message on the queen's window, "Fain would I climb, yet fear I to fall." Delighted, the queen scratched a reply, "If thy heart fail thee, climb not at all." She had challenged him, and Raleigh responded to the challenge. He loved the risks of adventure. Here was a new realm—the world of love in the court—for him to explore. Fearlessly, he rose in court until he became the favorite of his queen.

Raleigh and His Wardrobe

When Raleigh first appeared at court, he was an officer of low rank with little money and no property or title to his name. The image that he chose to portray was quite different. With his meager earnings, Raleigh invested in expensive clothes that were tailored to show off his bold style. Huge collars of lace, a sweeping cloak, and jewel-studded coats gave the impression that he had a large fortune. His wardrobe was another example of Raleigh's daring: If he failed to gain acceptance at court, he would have had nothing left except his fancy clothes.

Durham

From a Drawing by Hollar

DURHAM HOUSE   SALISBURY

The three Houses above represented, stood on the banks of the Thames
...ied the spot called DURHAM YARD, now the ADELPHI, and was built by Ant.y Bec, Bish.p
erect...   ...d covered
ally   ...sion of
His s...   ...OUSE, and the Site

This picture of mansions along the Thames River in London
includes Durham House *(left)* which Queen Elizabeth gave to
Sir Walter Raleigh for use in 1583. It is from here that he
planned and organized his first expeditions to the New World.

Publish'd 30. Nov. 1808, by W.m Herbert, L...

Salisbury   Woster

In the Pepysian   Library at Cambridge

HONI SOIT QVI MALY PENSE

... HOUSE   WORCESTER   HOUSE.

... nearly adjoining each other. DURHAM HOUSE, the first ... in the Plate, occu...

... of Durham, as a town residence for the Bishops of that See.   SALISBURY HOUSE was ...

... the site of the present Salisbury and Cecil Streets. WORCESTER HOUSE, origi...

... the Earls of Worcester, Edw.ᵈ the last Earl of Worcester died here in 1627, ...

... alled BEAUFORT BUILDINGS.   The above View was taken about the year 1630.

... nd Rᵗ Wilkinson. Nº 58 Cornhill, London.

Raleigh had no wealth or status, so it was not easy for him to woo the queen. To be seen with her, he needed money and fine clothes. The queen provided the means for him. In 1582, for his successes in Ireland, Raleigh was named one of three governors of Munster, a large and fertile region in Ireland. For conquering the land, Raleigh was given the authority to farm it and to tax its inhabitants. In addition, the queen granted him the right to tax exported fabric. In this manner, Raleigh began to build his fortune.

In 1584, Queen Elizabeth knighted him, and he was thereafter called Sir Walter Raleigh. To keep him close to her, Queen Elizabeth granted him the right to live in Durham House, a fine mansion along the Thames River in London. The men of his native Devon saw how quickly Raleigh was moving up in the eyes of the queen. In 1584, they elected him to Parliament to represent their town.

Raleigh had a fortune, a large piece of land, a title, a home, and an elected office. In the span of nine years, he had acquired unbelievable success for a common-born man. His great success was mostly due to the love of the queen, and to her he promised his undying love.

Restless Raleigh

But Raleigh was restless. A man of considerable energy and ambition, he longed to explore more of the world and to engage in great battles for the glory of England. While he explored the world of the court, he watched the battlefield successes of others, like his half brother, Sir Humphrey Gilbert.

In 1578, Gilbert acquired a patent that gave him the right to explore the New World and conquer it in the name of the queen. That same year, Raleigh and his half brother set out to enforce their patent by removing the Spanish from territories in the West Indies. Ten ships with supplies for a year left England, and in the Atlantic Ocean they engaged in a battle with the Spanish. Defeated, Raleigh and Gilbert managed to straggle back to England by May of 1579. Humiliated, Gilbert wanted revenge. In 1583, he assembled a new fleet and led an expedition to the New World, while Raleigh was kept at home by Queen Elizabeth. Gilbert was lost at sea.

The following year, Raleigh convinced the queen that he was the man to finish Gilbert's adventure. He was her knight in shining armor, and she awarded him the patent to conquer the New World. But the patent came at a cost. The queen forbade her lover from going on the explorations. Over the years, it became a source of frustration for Raleigh. He is credited as the "discoverer" of Virginia, which he named for the Virgin Queen, Elizabeth, (so called because she never married or bore children). However, he personally never set foot on the continent of what we now call North America.

Benoist sculp.

ROBERT DEVEREUX Earl of ESSEX.

The last of Queen Elizabeth I's favorites, Robert Devereux was presented before her court at a young age. Although he was twenty-one years old and she was fifty-four, Elizabeth indulged in many flirtations with him. The hot tempered Devereux had many quarrels with Raleigh and the queen. While her affection for him was genuine, it was probably like the love of a mother for a son.

Lord Essex

In the same year that Raleigh acquired the patent, Robert Devereux, the earl of Essex, appeared at court. Here was a bold upstart, a brash twenty-one-year-old who would not be tamed. As good-looking as Raleigh, Essex was born into a noble family. In the eyes of the queen, the earl of Essex began to glow brighter and brighter.

With a new rival at court, Raleigh's campaigns in the New World became very important. Raleigh needed a huge conquest for his queen in order to keep his station by her side. As he became better at playing the role of the gentleman at court, Raleigh used his position and the gifts from the queen to create a new role for himself as a merchant of the New World.

4

SEEKING FORTUNES IN THE NEW WORLD

To seek new worlds, for gold, for praise, for glory,
To try desire, to try love severed far,
When I was gone she sent her memory
More strong than were ten thousand ships of war
To call me back, to leave great honour's thought,
To leave my friends, my fortune, my attempt,
To leave the purpose I so long had sought,
And hold both cares and comforts in contempt.
                    —From Sir Walter Raleigh's "Ocean to Cynthia"

From 1584 until his death, Raleigh spent his fortune trying to take the New World from Spain. Since the queen would not let him lead these early expeditions, Raleigh instead became the organizer and supplier of the New World colonies, the merchant who would capture the continent for England.

England was very late to the game of exploring the New World. Spain and Portugal had already built cities, ports, and forts to defend themselves against native peoples and other European countries.

Raleigh's charms earned him enormous royal favors from Queen Elizabeth. These included vast lands in Ireland, tax, funds on fabric exports, and rights to sell wine. The money from these gifts funded an expedition to the New World.

In the face of the Spanish and Portuguese, Raleigh was daring enough to stake an English claim in the New World. Yet it would take time. Elizabeth and her advisers ordered that England would not attempt to colonize any place where a Christian king had taken possession. It was smart thinking. Angering Spain or Portugal could spell immediate doom to a tiny English colony. Raleigh knew that Spain and Portugal meant to keep the New World to themselves. He had to proceed carefully.

England Arrives in the New World

On April 27, 1584, Raleigh waved good-bye to two barks (ships) setting sail from England for the New World. Their mission was to explore unclaimed territory and plant crops as an experiment. The two ships reached the West Indies and proceeded northward until they landed at Wokoken Island, off present-day North Carolina, on July 2, 1584. A tribe of Indians saw the ship and approached peacefully. The British traded a tin cup for twenty deerskins, then planted crops and claimed the land for the queen of England. When they left, two Indians, Manteo and Wanchese, went with them.

In England, Raleigh and his captains used the presence of the natives to spread the news of the bountiful harvest in the New World. They generated considerable excitement, and in April 1585 an expedition of about 1,000 people left for Virginia.

The First Roanoke Expedition

The people on the expedition were an odd mixture. Many were hired by Raleigh to assess the value of the New World as a resource. Sir Richard Grenville, Raleigh's cousin, was leader of the expedition and captain of the *Tiger*, a ship that belonged to the queen. Others included Ralph Lane, a soldier who would become governor of the colony; Simon Fernandez, a Spanish pilot and navigator; Thomas Hariot, a brilliant mathematician and mapmaker; and John White, an artist. Grenville viewed the trip as an opportunity to attack the Spanish. Lane considered it a soldier's mission. Hariot and White were fascinated with the people and the culture of the New World. Together, these men and their varied goals created confusion among the leaders of the expedition.

Grenville led the expedition into the West Indies, where he played pirate against Spanish galleons for too long. This mistake was made worse when Fernandez ran the *Tiger* onto shore and spilled wheat and salt that could not be replaced. When the expedition finally landed as Manteo's guest at Roanoke Island in July, it had only twenty days of food left, few seeds to plant crops, and no time to grow anything.

45

Engraved for Middleton's Complete System of Geography.

SIR WALTER RALEIGH ordering the STANDARD of Queen Elizabeth to be erected on the Coast of VIRGINIA.

Taylor delin.   Sculp.

Nevertheless, the group decided to stay through the winter on that flat island battered by summer storms. In the sandy soil they planted a few crops from home, which did not grow well. The Indians had barely enough for their own people and little extra to share. A decision had to be made.

In September, a small rescue party set sail for England, leaving Lane behind with 108 men under his command. Lane's experience with colonies came from his work in Ireland, where the English were constantly battling the native people. By spring, Lane detected hostility from the Indians and learned that Wingina, a powerful chief, was planning to attack the colony. Before Wingina could attack, Lane attacked him, and one of his soldiers returned in triumph with the chief's severed head.

A few months later, Sir Francis Drake landed to resupply the colony just as a terrible storm arrived. Facing multiple dangers, Drake and Lane decided that it was time for all to return to England, and they set sail on June 18, 1586. To Lane, the expedition was a failure. To White and Hariot, who had spent considerable time with the Indians, it was a tremendous success, one that would come to haunt White in time.

This engraving, now in the National Maritime Museum, shows Raleigh planting the English flag in Virginia and is untrue to history. Although Raleigh organized and financed New World expeditions, he never set foot in North America.

This image of Native Americans cooking fish is from a painting by John White, whom Raleigh hired to make drawings on the expedition to Virginia. According to historians, White's images provide a remarkably accurate picture of Indian culture in the Carolina region at the time.

The Second Roanoke Expedition

Raleigh received these mixed reports and considered his options. Two expeditions had returned with little of financial value. But White and Hariot had made great discoveries. In addition to describing the natives and their way of life, they had come upon Chesapeake Bay. This site was intriguing to Raleigh, as a large, deep harbor could be a good place from which to launch attacks against the Spanish. By returning home with some captured Spanish goods and gold, the expedition had proved the value of piracy. Raleigh began to plan another expedition.

He had a couple of problems, however. In 1587, Queen Elizabeth appointed him her captain of the guard. It was a great honor but paid nothing and required him to be very close to her. Secondly, tensions between Spain and England were drifting toward war. Raleigh and all available ships were needed to defend the island. To Elizabeth, the New World was an afterthought.

But Raleigh refused to give up on his dream of exploring and conquering it for his queen. He turned to John White and Simon Fernandez, asking them to found another colony in the Chesapeake Bay with the name "Raleigh." In Raleigh's colony, people would live freely among the Indians. White shared Raleigh's dream, and brought along his pregnant daughter, Elenor, and her husband, Anias Dare. Their expedition set sail in the

SECOTAN

Dasamonquepeuc

Roanoac

Hatorasck

This engraving illustrates the arrival at Roanoke Island, Virginia, in 1585, of the expedition Raleigh sent to the New World.

The manner of their attire and painting themselues when they goe to their generall huntings or at theire Solemne feasts.

summer of 1587 for the New World under the navigation of Simon Fernandez.

Fernandez, alas, was more of a pirate than an explorer. He spent considerable time in the Caribbean attacking Spanish merchant ships. White grew angry with him but could not persuade him to head for the Chesapeake Bay. When the expedition finally arrived in July at Roanoke to check on the abandoned colonists, Fernandez claimed that he could go no further, as he needed to return to the Caribbean to continue pirating. For some reason, White accepted this explanation, and the English colonists found themselves once again abandoned on Roanoke Island. Their resupply ships, however, were expecting them to be in the Chesapeake area. The colonists decided that someone must return to England to inform Raleigh of the change of plans. That person, it was decided, would be John White.

John White returned to England, leaving his daughter, son-in-law, and granddaughter at Roanoke. With Raleigh's help, White struggled to put together a relief expedition to resupply the colony. Yet in the following year, war broke out with the Spanish, and any hope of getting ships supplied and under sail for the New World disappeared.

This portrait by John White shows a member of one of the two Algonquian Indian tribes that lived in what are now the states of Virginia and North Carolina. According to White's inscription, the man's body is painted for a special occasion. He wears a deerskin apron kilt, feathers in his hair, and copper beads around his neck and wrist. He holds a six-foot bow, and has a quiver made of rushes slung across his back. The quiver is tied by a puma's tail, which hangs down the man's back.

This painting by John White illustrates native people of the Secotan tribe holding a festival to celebrate the corn harvest at the end of summer. Ten men and seven women dance around a circle of posts carved with human heads, which may represent deities (gods). Three women clasp each other in the center of the circle. The dancers hold gourd rattles and leafy twigs, and some have painted their bodies.

White did manage to put two small ships to sea in April 1588, but they were attacked by French pirates, who took everything and left them with only one ship in which to sail back to England. When White finally arrived at Roanoke on August 16, 1590, there were no signs of a colony. There was no smoke, no boats on shore, and no people. The camp was deserted. His own possessions were spoiled and rotten. On the bark of one tree were carved the letters "CRO." According to a previous agreement, this secret code meant that the colonists had gone to Croatoan, which was an Indian settlement governed by Manteo, a friend to the English.

White never made it to Croatoan. His ships were in bad shape and the captains had lost many men getting to America. Neither captain would take White in search of the colonists and his family. They were never found. What became of the lost colony of Roanoke? No one knows. John White returned to England and never set foot in the New World again.

For Raleigh the merchant, the colonies of the New World were a financial disaster. However, he would be given the chance to rise once again, as the defense against the Spanish Armada would demand his abilities as a fleet commander.

This map shows the Virginia coast, which Raleigh continued to search for his lost colony. In 1602, he sent an expedition that landed near Croatoan Island, but it was unable to find the lost colonists. After the Jamestown settlement was established in Virginia in 1607, the Virginia colonists tried to find out from the natives what happened to the Roanoke settlers. However, they heard only rumors. The story of the lost colonists became legend in England, and their fate remains a mystery to this day.

5

DEFEAT OF THE SPANISH ARMADA AND THE NEW EMPIRE

He could never be connected with an enterprise which he was not determined to direct.
—Earl of Northumberland, referring to Sir Walter Raleigh

For England and Raleigh, the threat of the massive Spanish fleet continued to grow through the 1580s. Spain under King Philip II had colonized the New World, and his war chest was growing large with gold from trade in New World spices and materials. When his wife, Queen Mary, was succeeded by Elizabeth, King Philip had sworn that he would return England to the Catholic Church. Spain was just a short sail from the southern shores of England, and by 1586, war between the two countries was a matter of time. The political lines separating these nations were stark and immovable; Catholic and Protestant would soon battle again.

Queen Elizabeth was eager to postpone the war. The huge Spanish fleet, the Armada, was a dangerous threat, and she did not have the ships to strike back at Spain. At best,

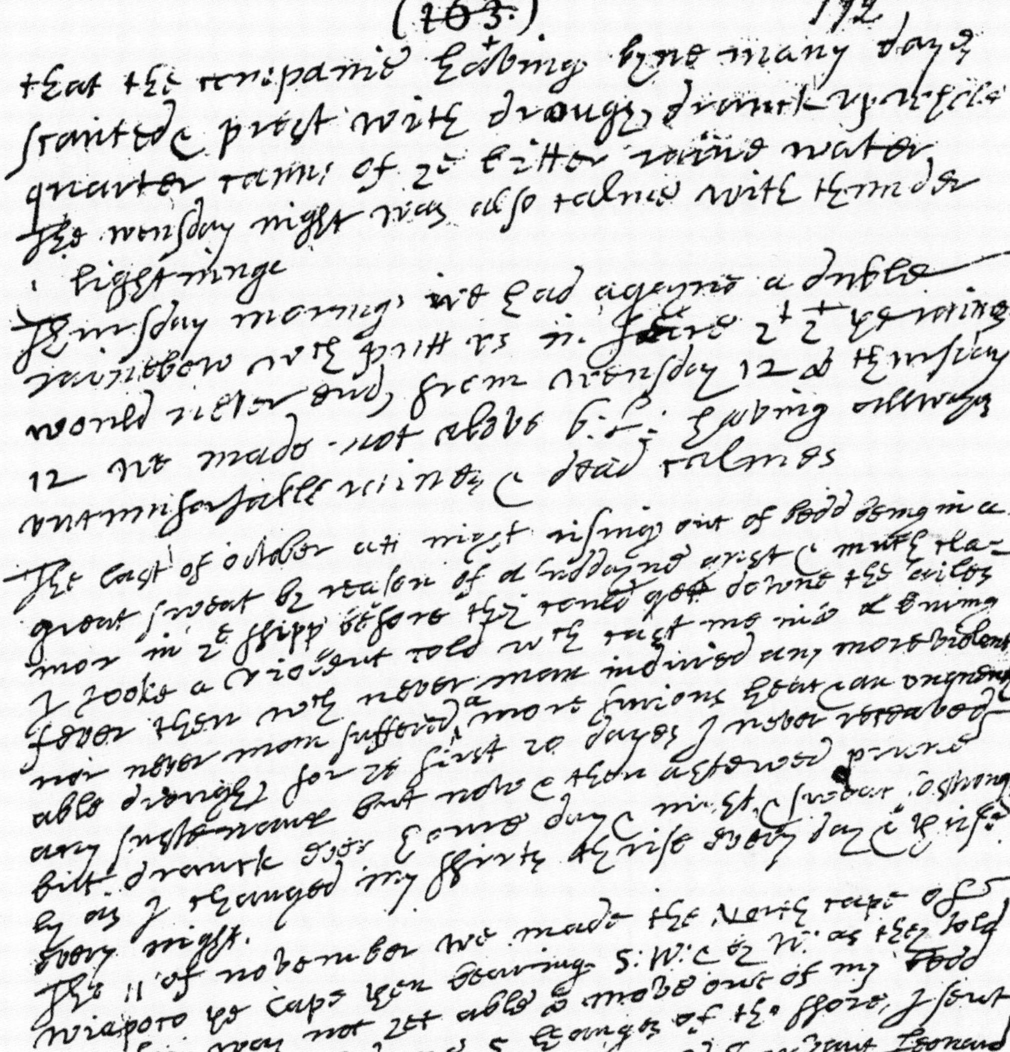
(163) 172

that the companie havinge bene many dayes straitened pinched with drought drank up the quarter canns of the bitter raine water. The wensday night was also calme with thunder & lightninge.

Thursday morning we had agayne a dubble rainebow which putt us in feare that the raine would never end. From wensday 12 to thursday 12 we made not above 6 L. having allwayes unconstant winds & dead calmes.

The last of October at night rising out of bedd being in a great sweat by reason of a sodayne gust & much clamor in the shipp before they could get downe the sailes I tooke a violent cold which cast me into a burning fever then which never man indured any more violent nor never man suffered a more furious heat & an unquenchable drought for the first 20 dayes I never receaved any sustenance but now & then a stewed prune but drank every houre day & night & sweat so strongly as I changed my shirts thrise every day & thrise every night.

The 11 of november we made the north cape of Wiapoco the cape then bearing S.W. & by W. as they told me for I was not yet able to move out of my bedd we rode in 6 fadome 5 leagues of the shore. I sent in my skiff to enquire for my old servant Leonard the Indian who had bene with me in England 3 or 4 yeares, the same man that tooke Mr Harcourts brother & 50 of his men when they came upon the coast & were in wonderfull distress, having neither meat nor meanes to live there but

In 1595, Raleigh set sail to find the fabled city of El Dorado. He penetrated 300 miles up the Orinoco River into the interior of Guiana, bringing home a few pieces of gold. Raleigh published this book of his adventure, *Discoverie of the Large, Rich and Bewtiful Empyre of Guiana*, the following year.

she could defend her land. If England lost the war, it was certain that Queen Elizabeth would lose her kingdom, her Church, and possibly her life. Against the Armada, the largest fleet assembled in history, the odds were against England, and Raleigh the commander had little time to rise to the challenge.

Raleigh's Fortunes Rise

By 1586, Raleigh had amassed a considerable fortune from the land taxes and patents that the queen had given him. He governed a massive tract of land in Ireland and had the right to tax a number of exported products. However, he would have to use that fortune in the fight against the Armada, for all of it had come from the queen of England.

Raleigh had other expeditions that required his time, energy, and funds. His first colony in America had been a failure, but he was planning a second expedition, scheduled to depart in 1587, the following year. His colonies in Ireland needed supplies and military support to protect against attacks from Irish rebels and possibly the Spanish. Raleigh had large responsibilities and grand plans.

The key to achieving his ambitious plans of exploration and conquest in the queen's name was to build his own fleet. Raleigh became actively involved in the design and building of his personal navy. The *Ark Ralegh* and the *Roebuck* were two barks of 200 tons each. His fleet also

Massive galleons, such as these, enabled explorers to travel far and succeed in sea battles. A Spanish design, they were slow but well-equipped for combat. The English bark, used for Raleigh's expeditions, was similar in design and strength.

included a number of pinnaces, two of which had captured the Spanish gentleman Don Pedro Sarmiento de Gamboa. Sarmiento related the story of a vast wilderness near the Amazon River in South America, an area that was later described as the site of El Dorado, the city of Incan gold. The tale fired Raleigh's considerable imagination and simmered there for ten years, until he could explore the empire of Guiana for himself.

Yet his foremost concern was preparing the fleet for attack on the Armada. His biggest ship was the *Ark Ralegh*. Built entirely to Raleigh's specifications, this 200-ton boat was bought by the queen of England for 5,000 pounds and became the flagship of the English navy in the war with the Spanish. It was "money well given" according to Lord Admiral Howard of Effingham, its first captain and admiral of the English fleet.

While Raleigh was a brave soldier and an experienced sailor, he was not to participate in the battle directly. In 1587, he had been named to the council to prepare for the coming war, yet the queen appointed him lieutenant general of Cornwall, meaning that he was responsible for training the first line of land defenses in southwestern England. Raleigh's success as a commander in France and Ireland and his popularity among the men of Cornwall made him the perfect soldier for the job. Unfortunately, events would keep him from the battle. His ships, though, were put to sea. Soon, they would be put to vigorous use.

The Spanish Armada

At a distance, the massive Armada was frightening to regard. Usually attacking in the formation of a crescent, it contained a total of 131 ships, including 20 galleons, 4 galleasses, and 44 heavily armed merchant ships. For years, King Philip II and his advisers had been developing a strategy for the attack on England. His massive fleet would engage the smaller, more nimble English ships and gain control of the English Channel. Then,

CHART OF THE ARMADA'S COURSE.
Pine's Engraving, 1739, of Tapestry then in House of Lords.

This map charts the course of the Spanish Armada on its invasion of England in 1588. According to the plan, the Armada would carry soldiers, equipment, and supplies from Spain to the Strait of Dover, win control of the English Channel, and protect the Duke of Parma's army as it crossed from the Netherlands to England. The joined armies would invade England and force Queen Elizabeth to agree to Spain's demands. However, foul weather and fast English ships foiled the plan.

from the Netherlands, the Duke of Parma's army of feared and battle-tested warriors would embark in barges to cross the channel to land on English soil without harassment from the English navy. These elite soldiers would overrun the English army and conquer the country.

Yet there was a flaw in the Spaniards' plan. The English navy was well-equipped to engage the Armada. For years, the English had been redesigning their ships so that they could sail almost directly into the wind. They had great maneuverability and could hold more ship-destroying cannons than the Spanish ships. Armed with long-range cannons, these quick ships could stand back from the Armada and blast them. In keeping their distance, the English ships could prevent the Armada vessels from throwing a grappling hook to stop them, board them, and conquer them. If the Spanish crews could not board the English ships, their ships could be torn to pieces. Both sides were aware of this flaw, and the English needed to exploit it to win the fight.

The Spanish Are Coming!

On July 19, 1588, a scout on the coast of England spied the dreaded crescent shape of the Spanish Armada far out to sea. He lit a flaming beacon, which signaled to the scouts north and south of him to light theirs. Soon, the entire coast knew that the Spanish were coming.

Naval Craft of Western Europe

In the age of exploration, across the North Atlantic, any of the following ships might be churning towards adventure, battle, and riches:

Galley: A design from the Middle Ages, the galley was a combination of rowboat and sailboat. If the wind died, slaves could pick up oars.

Galleass: A larger, more modern version of the galley. This fast and deadly ship had three masts and was popular in the Mediterranean Sea.

Galleon: The battleship of the time could also function as a merchant ship. Square-rigged in the forward mast, and slow in the water, a galleon needed deep harbors to anchor.

Pinnace: A light ship for multiple purposes, often escorting a larger ship. A pinnace had two or three masts and a flat stern on which cannons could be mounted.

Bark: A large sailing warship with three or more masts.

Fireboat: When a boat had exceeded its useful life in the navy, it was sometimes turned into a fireboat. Under the cover of night, sailors positioned the boat close to an anchored fleet, sent it in the direction of the navy, set it on fire, and abandoned ship before it crashed into the targeted ships. Sometimes, the boats were packed with explosives.

PARTE OF

CORNEWALL

Saltashe

Low

Milbroke

S.t Michaels Ilande

Dodman point

Cam hed

E. die s Port

The Englishe fleete

WEST

NORTH

WEST   EAST

SOVTH

The Scale of Englishe miles
Roberte Adams author

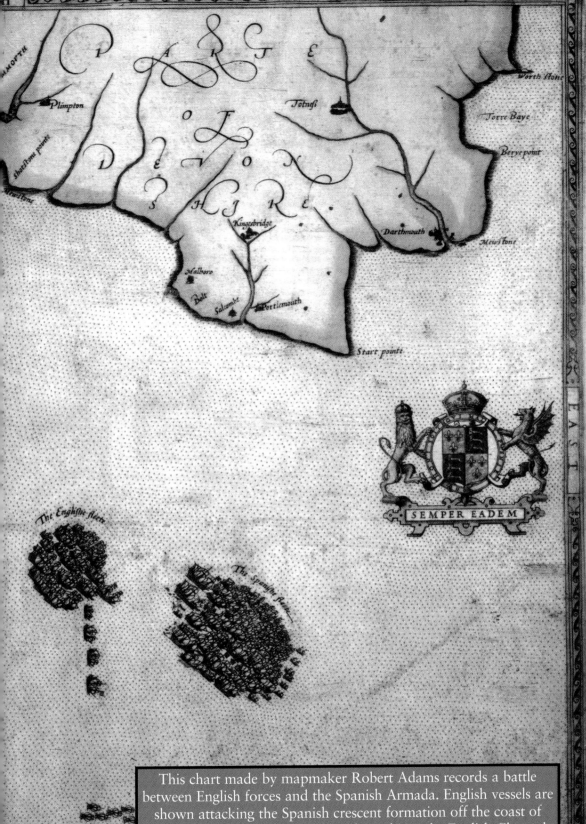

Plimpton

ShitStone pointe

MewStone

DEVONSHIRE

Totnes

Worth stone

Torre Baye

Berye point

Darthmouth

MewStone

Kingesbridge

Malbero

Bolt

Salcombe

Portlemouth

Start pointe

EAST

SEMPER EADEM

The Englishe fleete

The Spanish fleet

This chart made by mapmaker Robert Adams records a battle between English forces and the Spanish Armada. English vessels are shown attacking the Spanish crescent formation off the coast of Plymouth and pursuing them northward into the English Channel.

The Spanish fleet crawled along the coastline in full view of Raleigh and his untested troops on shore. The swift English ships were doing their best to harass the Spanish. Although the Spanish were frustrated by these pesky ships, the English did not do much damage. Wounded by cannon fire, yet unyielding, the dreaded crescent sailed onward, passing deepwater ports such as Plymouth, Portland, and the Isle of Wight. It became clear to all participants that the Spanish had to link up with the Duke of Parma's army; it was the key to everything.

The Armada reached the French port of Calais on July 27, 1588. The Catholic French provided a safe harbor for the Spanish. There, they would wait for the duke's army to arrive before both could cross the narrowest part of the channel to land at Dover, England, a mere twenty-one miles away. The English had to drive the Spanish navy out of this port, or they were doomed.

Under the cover of darkness on July 28, 1588, the English loaded a number of small boats and set them sailing for the anchored Spanish fleet. When those boats were set on fire, it must have been a terrifying sight to the Spanish. Were these fireboats loaded with explosives? There was no time to counter this threat, other than to cut their anchors and flee. The Spanish fleet scattered out into the channel, heading north. Little did the fleet commanders know that the pop and crackle coming from the boats was the sound of a few bullets and nothing more.

The mighty crescent had been broken. So used to working as one group, the scattered Armada was set upon by the captains of the English navy. Pushed northward along the east coast of England and into the North Sea, the Armada suffered terribly under massive storms that took fifty-six ships and countless lives. The Armada managed to sail around the north end of the British Isles and return to port in Spain. Reflecting later on the battle, King Philip II admitted, "I sent my ships to fight against men and not against the winds and waves of God. Even kings must submit to being used by God's will without knowing what it is." King Philip never returned England to Catholicism, and as he lay dying in 1598, he seemed to be finally at peace with his failure.

Raleigh witnessed the battle with the Spanish Armada from afar, for the queen wanted him safe and close to her. While his ships harassed and attacked the Armada, he stood with his troops waiting for the Duke of Parma's army, which never came. Although Raleigh the commander was out of the fight, circumstances would soon change, and he would be fighting for his honor, his family, and his life through his pen.

6

RALEIGH THE WRITER

For what we sometimes were, we are no more.
—From Sir Walter Raleigh's "Petition to Queen Anne"

With the defeat of the Armada in 1588, England rested and gained confidence in its growing power. England had established its place among the most powerful empires.

While others celebrated, Raleigh still had a number of problems. His colonies in Ireland struggled to produce income for him, and the American colony started by John White had been forsaken for years. His largest problem, though, was with the queen herself, and no sweet poem or love note could fix it.

The Other Elizabeth

As captain of the queen's guard, Raleigh was responsible for the personal safety of the queen and her ladies-in-waiting. A lady-in-waiting assisted the queen with personal matters, such as getting the queen dressed in

70

Raleigh's charm was as great in his writings as it was in his personality.
He wrote of love and desire:
"Passions are likened best to floods and streams:
The shallow murmur, but the deep are dumb."

her elaborate costumes. A lady-in-waiting was part of the inner circle of the court and was trusted with very private matters.

In protecting the queen, Raleigh found himself working closely with her ladies-in-waiting. A charmer and a flirt, Raleigh became very popular with them, and one in particular. In 1592, rumors began to swirl around the court that Raleigh had secretly married Elizabeth (Bess) Throckmorton, a nineteen-year-old lady-in-waiting, and had sneaked away with her to have a child. He forcefully denied it and continued to profess his love for Queen Elizabeth in sweet notes and poems to her. He raged that he was "alone, forsaken and friendless" because Elizabeth "is gone, she is lost." In such passionate writing, Raleigh hoped to bury the rumors under the outpourings of his heart.

The rumor, however, was true. Queen Elizabeth was furious. Her captain of the guard and one of her personal attendants had been having an affair behind her back. A jealous person, she felt betrayed by her old flame, Raleigh, and by one of her closest friends. She would not speak to Raleigh.

Raleigh was in deep trouble, for the land that he managed and the patents he taxed had been given to him by the queen. The queen's gifts provided the funds with which he could explore his grand dreams. She could take away all of these things in an instant. Without the queen's support, Raleigh had nothing.

Why did Raleigh risk so much to find love? Perhaps Lord Essex had driven him to do so. Since arriving at court in 1584, Essex had steadily become more and more popular with the queen and the other people at court. He was daring, brave, and handsome like Raleigh. He had some success on the battlefield. Unlike Raleigh, Essex was of noble blood. He was also much younger. Raleigh could not compete with that, and he found himself increasingly less important to the queen. He guarded the door to her private chambers, but more and more, it was Essex who was called into them.

It is just as likely, though, that Raleigh realized the value of true love. In Elizabeth Throckmorton he found a woman who would love him simply for the man he was. She did not love him so that he would conquer countries in her name. She did not love him because he charmed her with clever poems and gifts. She loved him purely and simply, and did so for the remainder of his life. To Raleigh, she was a source of great strength.

The Punishment

When Queen Elizabeth discovered the secret lovers, she placed them under house arrest at Durham House, the London home that she had provided for Raleigh. Raleigh and his Elizabeth were prisoners in their own home.

However, Raleigh did not sit idly. The love, despair, and anger in his heart came pouring out of his pen. All of the riches and success in his life could be attributed to Queen Elizabeth. In the jail of his own home, he began writing a poem to her. In "Ocean to Cynthia," he struggled to win her back through words, yet he found those words empty. In summary of his love for Queen Elizabeth, he wrote, "Twelve years entire I wasted in this war." The poem did not succeed.

The pride that had allowed him to dare to push closer to the queen would now become his undoing. His many enemies in court would turn to laugh as he fell from grace. Yet, in his writing, he did not lash out against his enemies or the queen. Rather, he realized that the responsibility for the ups and downs in his life were his and his alone.

In his poetry, Raleigh did not spare himself. He was able to see the lie behind every bow he had given over those twelve years. For his love of the queen was mixed and confused with his desire to rise in the world. Raleigh learned the hard way that love and desire are not the same thing. Yet as a result of this lesson in love, he found grace and true love.

Soon, Raleigh's finances began to crumble. In 1592, one of his ships managed to capture the Spanish galleon *Madre de Dios*, the largest ship in the world. This boat was laden

The desk in Raleigh's room in the Tower of London where he was imprisoned for twelve years by King James.

with 537 tons of valuable trade, such as silver, gold, ivory, pearls, and silks from the New World. As it sat in the port of Devon, bits of its valuable cargo began to disappear. Since she had a share of the cargo, the queen released Raleigh with the mission of going to Devon, retrieving the stolen cargo, and selling it for a profit. Raleigh accomplished this difficult task and delivered £78,000 profit to the queen. Yet, the money that he received from her did not even cover his expenses for putting his ships to sea. Raleigh was free from prison, but the queen was beginning to remove him from his fortune.

Raleigh was desperate to get back in the good graces of the queen, yet he was now aware of his difficult situation and diminished position in court. Into his speeches and writings came a tone of bitter realism and a sympathy for his fellow man. As a member of Parliament, he spoke up for the removal of taxes on the poorest people and against a bill that would have been very cruel to English Catholics. In his writings, he let his mind roam away from the court and to the larger issues of what it meant to be a human being. And his mind did return to the story told to him by the captured Spaniard, Don Sarmiento—the story of El Dorado. No longer required to be close to the queen, Raleigh dreamed more and more of finding the fabled golden city.

7

THE SEARCH
FOR EL DORADO

*[B]eing all driven to lie in the rain and weather, in the open air,
in the burning sun, and upon the hard boards . . . with the most
wet clothes of so many men thrust together and the heat of the
sun, I will undertake that there was never any prison in England
that could be found more unsavoury and loathsome.*
— From Sir Walter Raleigh's *The Discoverie of the Large,
Rich and Bewtiful Empyre of Guiana*

El Dorado did exist. In Spanish, *El Dorado* means "the Golden Man." A generation before Raleigh was born, a story began to emerge from the South American jungle of a naked Chibcha king who was covered in gold. A sophisticated civilization in the area that is now Colombia, the Chibcha performed a ritual in which their king was covered with a sticky resin, sprayed with golden dust and set across a sacred lake in a raft. The king then jumped into the lake, spreading this fine gold across the surface. This story was repeated by a number of explorers and is considered to be true to this day.

This sixteenth-century engraving plays on myths about gold in the fabled city of El Dorado. A Chibcha goldsmith is shown creating gold in a massive pot, while others pick up gold from the ground. In reality, the region's gold was not easy to find.

It was an old story, however. Long before the arrival of Europeans in the New World, the Chibcha had ceased to perform the ritual. Over time, the story had grown into the myth of an entire city rich enough to cover its king in gold.

When Raleigh first heard the legend of El Dorado, it appealed to him for many reasons. The story itself was of a magical kingdom, hidden deep in the jungle of a faraway land. The journey to El Dorado would be a grand adventure, and finding it would be an epic conquest. Raleigh would become rich beyond his wildest dreams. He would also deliver a grand blow to Spanish ambitions in the New World and would secure his name among the greatest explorers in history.

In so doing, Raleigh would return to the good graces of the queen, for his problems at court had grown worse. In 1593, he had been accused of atheism for debating the existence of God at a dinner. After a long trial, Raleigh was acquitted in 1594. Given his bad name at court and the growing list of his enemies, the chances of him getting back to the queen's side were fading. He turned to the dream of El Dorado in earnest.

The First Voyage to El Dorado

In 1594, Raleigh began putting together his expedition. He sent one of his loyal captains, Jacob Whiddon, on an exploratory

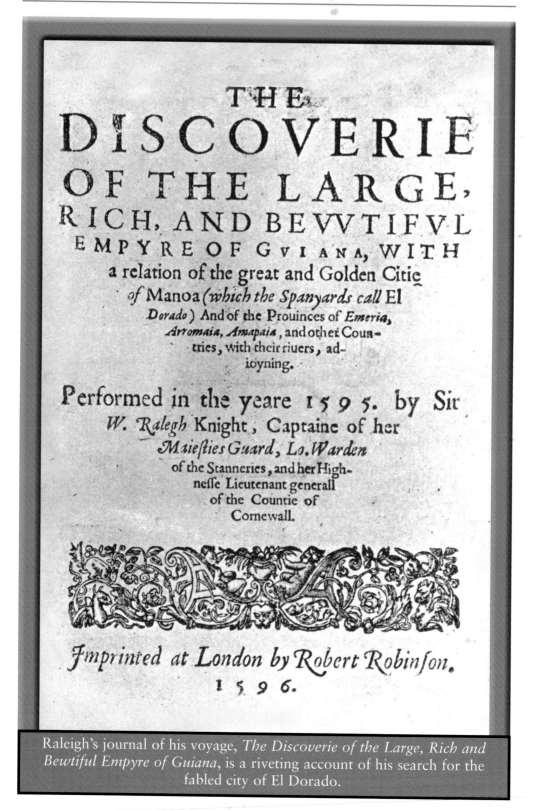

THE DISCOVERIE OF THE LARGE, RICH, AND BEVVTIFVL EMPYRE OF GVIANA, WITH

a relation of the great and Golden Citie of Manoa (*which the Spanyards call El Dorado*) And of the Prouinces of *Emeria, Arromaia, Amapaia*, and other Countries, with their riuers, adioyning.

Performed in the yeare 1595. by Sir W. *Ralegh* Knight, Captaine of her *Maiesties Guard*, Lo. Warden of the Stanneries, and her Highnesse Lieutenant generall of the Countie of Cornewall.

Imprinted at London by Robert Robinson.
1596.

Raleigh's journal of his voyage, *The Discoverie of the Large, Rich and Bewtiful Empyre of Guiana*, is a riveting account of his search for the fabled city of El Dorado.

mission. Whiddon was greeted warmly by Don Antonio de Berrío, the ruling Spaniard in Trinidad, the island guarding the mouth of the Orinoco River. However, when Whiddon began to ask questions of the local Indians about the existence of El Dorado, Berrío panicked and killed eight of Whiddon's men.

When Whiddon returned to England with his tale, Raleigh sought and received letters of patent from the queen to explore and conquer the Orinoco River Delta. These letters were much stronger than those he had received for North America. He was authorized to attack and enfeeble any Spanish forces within 200 leagues of his settlement. "Our servant Sir Walter Raleigh" was allowed to take any Spanish treasure that he could.

Into such a grand opportunity, Raleigh sank his entire fortune and appointed himself the admiral of his fleet of four ships. On February 6, 1595, the fleet took to sea. Landing at Trinidad in April, Raleigh succeeded in capturing Berrío. From him, Raleigh received confirmation of the El Dorado legends. According to Raleigh's journal of the adventure, *The Discoverie of the Large, Rich and Bewtiful Empyre of Guiana*, Berrío had made three difficult journeys into the jungle without success, yet he still was determined to find El Dorado. Learning of Raleigh's intentions, Berrío "was stricken into a great melancholy and sadness" according to Raleigh, which further inspired the Englishman. Raleigh and Berrío saw the same dream in each other, which seemed to

This is an image of an old map of the northern coast of South America. Dwellings built by the native people of the area as well as boats and animals decorate the coastline.

BRASILIA.

Salinas Car.
Varedema
R. Upanema
R. Laguariba
R. Parigura
Propea
Coco
Pirangi
Povo de Siara
R. Canigui
R. Mondalag
R. de Cruz
Satiba Rio
Tortugas
S. Francisco R.
R. Mandabig
R. Penema
R. Taguraon
R. Guaroßa
R. Para
R. Cumorchig
R. Aperegi
R. Tagi
Tauca
Olbapam
Roq
Itaiba
R. Commana
R. de S. Marçal
R. de S. Paulo
R. Flaman.
R. Domilo
Coſta de L.

R. Lucas
R. Hiapon
R. Araabiguit ais
Iguap
Camuçu
Ototry
I. Coragu
C. Blanco
I. Grab...
re...

MAR Æquinoctial.

BRASILIA
Sept.
AMAZONES
ORINOQVE

DE

50   100
Horæ itineris.

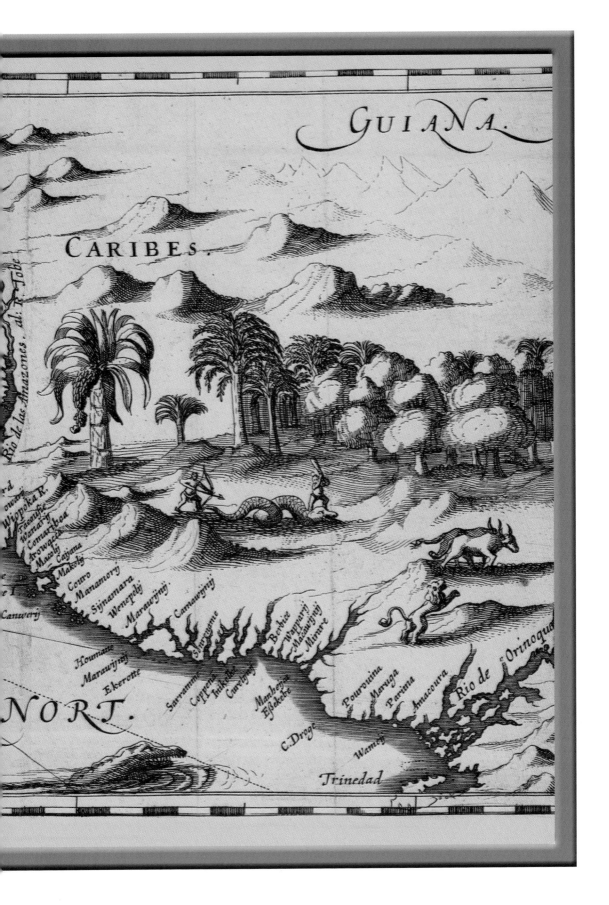

be proof of its validity for both men. Soon, Raleigh and his party were heading inland up the river.

But was it the right river? The Orinoco Delta is a vast plain of waterways and swampland, the navigation of which was known only to the local Indians. Yet Raleigh shied away from forcing the natives to help him. It was very important to him that when dealing with the natives, no one in his party take so much as a piece of fruit without paying them. When one of his men was killed by a local chieftain, Raleigh did not respond violently, instead capturing one of the chief's men to serve as a guide upriver.

The trip was very difficult on Raleigh and his men, who suffered from the extreme heat and humidity. Raleigh had to plead, shame, and threaten his men to keep rowing. Through beautiful country with "birds of all colors, some carnation, some crimson . . . and all other sorts both simple and mixed," as Raleigh wrote, the expedition penetrated farther into this land of mystery. Brilliant flowers dappled the dense jungle of the riverbank. Strange animals peeked through the undergrowth and, startled, disappeared into it. Raleigh noted, ". . . for [alligators], it exceeded, for there were thousands of these ugly serpents." One of them ate a sailor. Though the land was gorgeous, the adventure was trying.

Near exhaustion, the men saw four canoes paddling away from them. Giving chase, they discovered the canoes on an embankment and a set of Spanish refiner's tools, used to remove gold from rock, in the brush. Raleigh grew more excited. A few days later, according to *The Discoverie of the Large, Rich and Bewtiful Empyre of Guiana*, Raleigh encountered an old man who told a fragmented tale from his youthful days:

> There came down into that large valley of Guiana, a nation from so far off as the Sun slept . . . with so great a multitude as they could not be numbered nor resisted . . . and had now made themselves Lords of all . . . built a great town . . . and therein the great king . . . kept three thousand men to defend the borders . . .

Raleigh took these scraps of evidence as proof of the golden city. Shortly thereafter, he turned at the junction of the Orinoco and Caroni Rivers and headed back to England.

There are many beautiful passages in Raleigh's book on the exploration of Guiana. In them, Raleigh describes an untouched and precious land that would be of great value to the English. His tale is a fascinating read and, when published in 1596, it became a success all over Europe.

The queen, however, was not impressed. She was perhaps occupied with the intrigues at court, for she was getting old and had no heir. Who would sit on the throne after Elizabeth? Would that person be an enemy or an ally to Raleigh? With so many enemies at court, Raleigh had to quickly learn the rules of this game, or his rivals would get the new monarch to bring him down.

8

THE SECOND VOYAGE
TO EL DORADO

What shall become of me now, I know not; I am unpardoned in England, and my poor estate consumed ... I desire your Honour to hold me in your good opinion, and ... to take some pity on my poor wife, to whom I dare not write, for the renewing of her sorrows for her son.
—Sir Walter Raleigh, writing to Secretary Winwood, on the deaths of his son and Sir Lawrence Keymis on the second voyage to Guiana

Raleigh was not able to return to Guiana for a long time. He was again diverted into the war with Spain. In 1596, Raleigh, Lord Admiral Howard, and Raleigh's rival Lord Essex led an attack on the Spanish port city of Cádiz. But the men did not get along. Although only four Spanish galleons were at Cádiz to defend the forty merchant ships in the harbor, none of the English captains allowed the others to lead the battle. Separately, they defeated the four galleons and shore protections. Fighting bravely despite an injury, Raleigh won the queen's appreciation again, but the victory was somewhat empty. Rather than let the English acquire their treasure, the Spanish sunk the entire merchant fleet.

This image illustrates Raleigh's march along the Orinoco River in Guiana. From the shores of the river, Raleigh could see the peak of Cerro Duida; according to the native people of the region, El Dorado lay beyond.

In 1597, Raleigh returned to Queen Elizabeth's court as her captain of the guard, but by the turn of the century, the queen's court was fading. She was aging and had not decided who would be her successor. Without a direct heir, the political intrigue to find the next monarch of England began. As Raleigh sought to regain favor with his queen, he wondered how to plan a future with the next monarch. In this game of intrigue, Raleigh played the role of politician. Ultimately, he was not a good one.

Who Will Lead England?

The struggle to decide who would lead England in the seventeenth century was very complicated. While many candidates were discussed, the leading competitor was King James VI of Scotland. James was related to Elizabeth's grandfather, King Henry VII. Elizabeth continually delayed her decision.

King James was confident, however. From Scotland, he began to test the alliances of the various lords at court. Particularly dangerous to him was the earl of Essex. If circumstances allowed, Essex himself might claim the throne. While he enjoyed the privileges of his closeness with the queen, she may have seen Essex as a threat. He was on dangerous ground and had to step lightly. A light step, however, was not Essex's style. While he was popular with the queen, his men, and the people of England, he was ill-suited for this game of politics.

Like Raleigh, Essex desperately sought to secure his position through glory on the battlefield. He led an attack against the Spanish at Fayal in 1597 that was largely unsuccessful. This expedition is known as "The Islands Voyage." Essex then led a campaign in 1599 against Irish rebels, but failed to put them down. Disgraced, Essex made a truce with the Irish, which he had no right to do. He hurried back to England and, dirtied with travel and battle, presented himself to the queen in her private chambers. Alarmed at his brashness, she banished him from London. In 1601, Essex and his men attempted a coup against her. Under Raleigh's leadership, Essex was captured and executed.

Many blamed Raleigh for scheming to bring down Essex, and in some ways, it was true. Yet Raleigh remained loyal to his queen. With the death of Essex, the way was paved for King James to succeed Elizabeth. One of King James's servants inquired if Raleigh would meet with the king of Scotland. As a sign of respect to Elizabeth, Raleigh refused. Other Englishmen deviously informed the king that Raleigh was not to be trusted.

On March 24, 1603, Queen Elizabeth died. Her reign had been longer than any monarch in memory, and she had been dearly loved by her people. Her legacy was to have beaten back the Spanish and to have led England from an island to an empire. Yet no future had been secured for Raleigh.

Sir Walter Raleigh

King James I of England *(above)* was born in 1566 to Mary, Queen of Scots and her second husband, Henry Stewart, Lord Darnley. James ascended the Scottish throne in 1567. He was later named successor to the English throne by his cousin, Elizabeth I, and ascended that throne after her death in 1603. After ruling Scotland for fifty-eight years and England for twenty-two years, he died of a stroke in 1625.

When King James took the throne, he immediately showed his displeasure with Raleigh, the daring adventurer for Queen Elizabeth. Raleigh was stripped of his valuable monopolies and patents. He was removed from Durham House. At a royal hunt at Windsor Castle, Raleigh was trapped by the king's men and imprisoned in the Tower of London. After 1603, Raleigh was never again a truly free man.

Twelve Years in the Tower

During this confusing time, Raleigh had made a new ally in Lord Cobham. A wealthy noble, Cobham became involved in a plot to overthrow James. When he was caught, Cobham claimed Raleigh had been part of the plot. Raleigh was charged with treason.

Raleigh's trial was big news at the time, and in representing himself, he was magnificent at center stage. He argued the meaning of treason and debated against Sir Edward Coke, the finest lawyer for the Crown. During the trial, Cobham gave conflicting testimony about Raleigh's role, and was unreliable in court. Although Raleigh fought bravely with words and won the public's heart, the court found him guilty of treason and sentenced him to death.

The English public was in an uproar over this news from their new king. King James had changed many things that the popular Elizabeth had established. Now he was going to kill one of her greatest champions. Seeing an opportunity to win the favor of the people, King James pardoned Raleigh and spared his life.

Raleigh, however, was still a prisoner of King James. For the next decade, he would remain in the Tower of London while he worked on his tome, *The Historie of the World*, and tutored the son of King James, Prince Henry. But Prince Henry caught a fever in 1612 and died. With him went Raleigh's hope for freedom.

The Doomed Voyage

After the death of his son, King James began to have financial difficulties. Typically, the king of England raised money by asking Parliament, which had the power to tax, for funds. But King James refused to stoop to this. Raleigh played on the king's desire for gold to rekindle the quest of El Dorado. After much lobbying, the king agreed to let Raleigh sail for Guiana under two restrictions: He must return with gold, and he was not to harm the Spanish. Raleigh's situation seemed nearly impossible: He was to get gold from a region that the Spanish guarded and had searched for for many years, but he was forbidden to turn pirate and steal it from them.

Raleigh leapt at the chance. On June 12, 1617, thirteen ships and 1,000 men set sail under Raleigh's command. On the lead ship *Destiny* sailed Raleigh,

This modern map shows the route Raleigh took on his voyages to El Dorado.

Caribbean Sea

72   68   64   60

Martinique
(FR.)

Fort-de-France ☆

SAINT LUCIA ★ **Castries**

SAINT VINCENT AND
THE GRENADINES

Kingstown ■   BARBADO
                          Bridgetown

Saint
George's ★ GRENADA

Aruba
(NETH.)   Netherlands
               Antilles
Oranjestad ☆ (NETH.)
   Aruba   Curaçao Bonaire
     Willemstad ☆

uerto
co

olivar

Golfo
de
Venezuela

Punto
Fijo

Coro ∙

Riecito ∙

FALCÓN

racaibo
○

ZULIA

Cabimas ∙

Lago
de
Maracaibo

Barquisimeto ∙

Valera ∙

TRUJILLO

Mérida
MÉRIDA

TÁCHIRA
San
Cristóbal

El Amparo ∙
              Arauca

Puerto
Cabello ○
San
Felipe ○ Valencia ○
LARA
         Maracay ●
Los Teques ●

Guanare ∙
PORTUGUESA

Barinas ∙

BARINAS

Río Apure

APURE

San
Fernando ∙

San Juan
de los
Morros

GUÁRICO

San
Carlos ∙
COJEDES

Río

Isla la
Tortuga

NUEVA
ESPARTA

Isla de
Margarita

La Asunción ∙

Caracas ★ La Guaira ∙

Cumaná ∙

Barcelona ∙

Maturín ∙

SUCRE

Güiria ∙

Port-of-Spain ★

Tobago

TRINIDAD AND
TOBAGO

Trinidad

Gulf
of
Paria

NORTH
ATLANTIC
OCEAN

MONAGAS

Tucupita ∙

ANZOÁTEGUI

Curiapo ∙

DELTA
AMACURO

Ciudad
Guayana ∙

Port
Kaitun

Cabruta ∙

Río Orinoco

Caicara ∙

El Jobal ∙
El iron
mine

Puerto
Carreño ∙

Puerto
Ayacucho ∙

San Juan
de Manapiare ∙

San Fernando
de Atabapo ∙

Puerto
Inírida ∙

Río Meta

OLOMBIA

Río Guaviare

José del
uaviare

Río Guainía

AMAZONAS

Esmeralda ∙

Río Casiquiare

Ciudad
Bolívar ∙

Ciudad
Piar ∙

La Paragua ∙

BOLÍVAR

Canaima ∙

Río Caura

Río Caroní

El
Dorado ∙

Guasipati ∙

Bochinche ∙

Tumeremo ∙

Matthews
Ridge

GUYAN

Peters Mine

Issano

Santa Elena
de Uairén ∙

Orindu

Normandia ∙

Vila Brasil ∙

Bonfim ∙

Leth

Boa Vista ∙

Río Orinoco

São Gabriel
da Cachoeira ∙

Cucuí ∙

Río Negro

Río Branco

Novo
Paraíso ∙

BRAZIL

Río Japurá

Río Uraricoera

Repr
Bal

Bali

Amazon

68   64

| | 1st expedition | 1595 |
| | 2nd expedition | 1617 |

Boundary representation is
not necessarily authoritative.

his old friend Lawrence Keymis, and Raleigh's son, Wat. En route Raleigh contracted a terrible fever and became too weak to lead the excursion inland. Instructed by his father to avoid the Spanish, Wat nevertheless attacked their fort at San Thome and was slain in the English victory. The remainder of the English troops scaled the walls of the fort and burned the fort and the town to the ground.

Raleigh was dejected, and he directed his rage at Keymis. Raleigh had lost a son and faced death at home, and still they had not found gold in the New World. Keymis and Raleigh's younger son, George, carried the final hopes of the expedition 300 miles upriver to no avail. Keymis returned to Raleigh and, upon making his report, took his own life with a knife. Raleigh wrote to his wife with the tragic news of their son's death:

> Comfort your heart . . . I shall sorrow for us both; and I shall sorrow the less because I have not long to sorrow, because not long to live . . . My brains are broken, and it is a torment to me to write . . . The Lord bless and comfort you, that you may bear patiently the death of your valiant son.

Equipped with a fleet of ships, Raleigh could have fled and turned pirate or returned to his old allies in France. Yet Raleigh chose to return to England to face certain death. Failing at the game of politics, Raleigh had one final role to play.

9

THE DEATH OF SIR WALTER RALEIGH

For whoso reaps renown above the rest
With heaps of hate shall surely be oppress'd.
—Sir Walter Raleigh, 1575

On June 21, 1618, Raleigh piloted the filthy *Destiny* into Plymouth harbor alone; all of his remaining ships had abandoned him. His wife, Elizabeth, was there to greet him and to share in his misery. A few days later, Vice Admiral Sir Lewis Stukeley, a distant cousin, arrived with orders from King James to arrest Sir Walter Raleigh.

Raleigh was kept in Plymouth for over a month as King James mulled over what to do. Upon hearing of the sacking of San Thome, the Spanish envoy to England demanded of the king that Raleigh be hanged in the central square in Madrid. Financially incapable of waging war against Spain and personally unwilling to resist, James gave his word to the envoy that Raleigh would receive severe punishment. Yet James knew that Raleigh, the last of the heroes of the Elizabethan Age, had gained popularity among the people. King James could not give him to the Spanish without

Raleigh awaits his beheading in the Old Palace Yard. Through his short-comings and his successes, Raleigh became an icon of the great adventurers who helped to establish the English empire.

suffering in the eyes of his people. Secretly, he may have hoped that Raleigh would try to escape.

When Raleigh was moved to the Tower of London, he did try to escape. His jailer and cousin, Sir Lewis Stukeley, arranged a false beard and passage for Raleigh to France. However, Raleigh's small boat was shadowed by a larger one across the channel, and he was caught before reaching the French coast. Stukeley had set him up.

In the Tower of London, Raleigh considered his fate. He had angered the king, violated strict orders, and attempted to escape. In facing death, however, Raleigh's spirit rose again. In his cell on the night before his execution, Raleigh recopied an old poem of his, adding two lines at the end:

> *Even such is time, which takes in trust*
> *Our youth, our joys, and all we have,*
> *And pays us but with age, and dust;*
> *Who in the dark and silent grave*
> *When we have wandered all our ways*
> *Shuts up the story of our days.*
> *And from which earth and grave and dust,*
> *The Lord will raise me up I trust.*

Raleigh the prisoner saw the arc of his life, how it had carried him so high yet would shortly render him to dust. His wife Elizabeth visited him on that final night and shared his fears and sadness for the fates of her and their son. At midnight, she kissed him for the last time and left.

On October 29, 1618, Raleigh was paraded to the scaffold. As in so many other dangerous moments in his life, he displayed rare courage. Seeing an old friend in the crowd, Raleigh took off his hat and gave it to the friend. According to Willard Mosher Wallace's *Sir Walter Raleigh*, he said, "Thou hast more need of it now than I." On the scaffold, he gave a stirring speech, defending his name, his actions, and his views. He held no grudges. In touching the executioner's ax, he found the humor to say, "This is sharp medicine, but it is a sure cure for all diseases." He knelt before the ax, and when the executioner hesitated before the great English hero, Raleigh shouted, "What dost thou fear? Strike, man strike!"

Thus ended the life of one of the most accomplished men in English history. Protestant, gentleman, merchant, commander, writer, explorer, and politician—Raleigh played all of these roles with equal boldness. In some, he found great success, yet his successes were often followed by swift and terrible failures. Raleigh, the upstart from the Devon countryside, had risen to the heights of Elizabethan society and, for his presumption, had been brought down to the humblest of ends. He fully engaged himself in each role that he played, exploring the possibilities and daring the impossible. If all the world's a stage, as his contemporary William Shakespeare wrote, then Sir Walter Raleigh was truly one of its grandest performers.

CHRONOLOGY

1554   Walter Raleigh is born in Devon, England.

1569   Raleigh sees his first military action in the Huguenot army in France under the Comte de Montgomerie. He fights bravely in fierce battles.

1575   Raleigh returns to England from France and begins training as a lawyer. He does not complete his studies.

1578   Raleigh departs with Sir Humphrey Gilbert in the first expedition against the Spaniards to enforce the English patent claims to the New World. They return defeated.

1580   Raleigh participates in a bloody massacre in Ireland that later shapes his thinking about how to deal with native populations in the New World.

1584   Raleigh appears in Queen Elizabeth's court. He gains the English patent to settle the New World, is knighted, and is elected to Parliament.

1584   Raleigh sponsors the first expedition to Roanoke, led by Amadas and Barlowe. The queen forbids him to go.

1585   Raleigh sponsors the second expedition to Roanoke, led by White, Grenville, Lane, and Hariot. The queen again forbids him to go.

1587   Raleigh gains land in Ireland and is appointed captain of the queen's guard.

1588   The English navy defeats the Spanish Armada.

1592   Raleigh marries Elizabeth Throckmorton in secret and they have a child. The angry Queen Elizabeth imprisons them in the Tower of London. Raleigh loses his station in the court.

1592   Raleigh's agents capture the Spanish galleon *Madre de Dios* and bring its massive cargo to England. Queen Elizabeth frees him from prison to secure and sell the cargo.

1594   Raleigh is charged with atheism and acquitted.

1595   Desperate to get in the queen's good graces again, Raleigh goes in search of El Dorado in Guiana.

1596 Raleigh publishes *The Discoverie of the Large, Rich and Bewtiful Land of Guiana*. Raleigh, Lord Essex, and Lord Charles Howard attack the Spanish Armada at Cádiz.

1597 Raleigh is re-appointed the captain of the queen's guard. He, Essex, and Admiral Howard fail to defeat the Spanish at Fayal.

1603 Raleigh is arrested, convicted of treason, and imprisoned in the Tower of London.

1603 Queen Elizabeth dies. Her cousin, King James of Scotland, is crowned king of England.

1615 Raleigh's *Historie of the World* is published and becomes popular across western Europe.

1616 Raleigh is released from the Tower of London.

1617 Raleigh, Wat Raleigh, and Lawrence Keymis sail for Guiana to find El Dorado. Raleigh contracts fever, Wat is killed, and Keymis commits suicide.

1618 Raleigh returns to England. He is arrested, attempts to escape, is captured, and dies nobly.

GLOSSARY

annul   To void; to end an agreement such as marriage.

Armada   Spanish for "navy."

atheism   The belief that there is no god or gods.

colonize   To settle a foreign land.

coup   An overthrow of a ruler.

courtier   Anyone close to the king or queen who advised and flattered them.

El Dorado   In Spanish, it means "the Golden Man." Spanish explorers described an Incan ritual in which a chief was sprayed in gold powder. It was believed that the location of this ritual was the legendary city of gold.

faction A subset of a group, army, or political party.

Huguenots French Protestants in the fifteenth and sixteenth centuries who rebelled against the Catholic majority in France.

monarch A person who reigns over a state or territory, usually for life and by hereditary right.

patent The right to develop an area such as the New World in the name of the Crown.

Renaissance A series of literary and cultural movements during the fourteenth, fifteenth, and sixteenth centuries, based on the concept of the value of the individual.

valiant Brave.

FOR MORE INFORMATION

The British Library
96 Euston Road
London NW1 2DB
UK
+44 (0)20 7412 7332
Web site: http://www.bl.uk

The British Museum
Great Russell Street
Bloomsbury
London, WC1B 3DG
UK
+44 (0)20 7323 8000
Web site: http://www.thebritishmuseum.ac.uk

British National Maritime Museum
Greenwich
London, SE10 9NF
UK
+44 (0)20 8858 4422
Web site: http://www.nmm.ac.uk

Fort Raleigh National Historic Site
1401 National Park Drive
Manteo, NC 27954
(252) 473-5772
Web site: http://www.nps.gov/fora/index.htm

The Lost Colony Theatre Under the Stars
1409 Highway 64/264
Manteo, NC 27954
(252) 473-3414
Web site: http://www.thelostcolony.org

Roanoke Island Festival Park
1 Festival Park
Manteo, NC 27954
(252) 475-1500
Web site: http://www.roanokeisland.com

Roanoke Island Visitors Center
Highway 64
Manteo, NC 27954
(252) 473-1144

Web Sites

Due to the changing nature of Internet links, the Rosen Publishing Group, Inc., has developed an online list of Web sites related to the subject of this book. This site is updated regularly. Please use this link to access the list:

http://www.rosenlinks.com/lee/wara/

FOR FURTHER READING

Aronson, Marc. *Sir Walter Raleigh and the Quest for El Dorado*. New York: Clarion Books, 2000.

Chippendale, Neil. *Sir Walter Raleigh: The Search for El Dorado*. New York: Chelsea House Publishers, 2001.

Korman, Susan, and Arthur Meier Schlesinger. *Sir Walter Raleigh: English Explorer and Author*. New York: Chelsea House Publishers, 2000.

Lacey, Robert. *Sir Walter Raleigh*. London: Phoenix Press, 2001.

Mattingly, Garrett. *The Armada*. Cambridge: Riverside Press, 1959.

Milton, Giles. *Big Chief Elizabeth: The Adventures of the First English Colonists in America*. New York: Farrar, Straus & Giroux, 2000.

BIBLIOGRAPHY

Adamson, J.H., and H.F. Folland. *The Shepherd of the Ocean*. Boston: Gambit, 1969.

Anniina Jokinen. "Sir Walter Ralegh (1552–1618)." June 13, 1996. Retrieved August 2001 (http://www.luminarium.org/renlit/ralegh.htm).

Anniina Jokinen. "Elizabeth I (1533–1603)." June 3, 1996. Retrieved August 2001 (http://www.luminarium.org/renlit/eliza.htm).

Aronson, Marc. *Sir Walter Raleigh and the Quest for El Dorado*. New York: Clarion Books, 2000.

Edwards, Philip. *Sir Walter Raleigh*. New York: Longmans, Green and Co., Inc., 1953.

Greenblatt, Stephen J. *Sir Walter Ralegh: The Renaissance Man and His Roles*. New Haven, CT: Yale University Press, 1973.

Paul Halsall. "Sir Walter Raleigh (1554–1618): The Discovery of Guiana, 1595." August 1998. Retrieved August 8, 2001 (http://www.fordham.edu/halsall/mod/1595raleigh-guiana.html).

Raleigh, Walter. *The Discoverie of the Large, Rich and Bewtiful Empyre of Guiana*. New York: Da Capo, 1968.

INDEX

About the Author

Steven P. Olson is a freelance writer who lives in Oakland, California, and likes to travel the world. His Web site is http://www.stevenolson.com.

Photo Credits

Series Design and Layout

Tahara Hasan

Editor

Christine Poolos